THE APERTURE HISTORY OF PHOTOGRAPHY SERIES

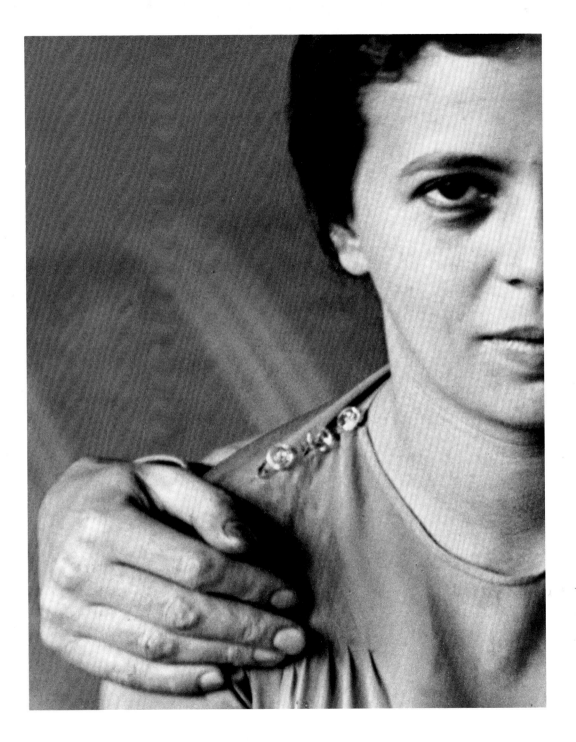

André Kertész

APERTURE

The History of Photography Series is produced by Aperture, Inc., under the artistic direction of Robert Delpire. *André Kertész* is the sixth book in the Series.

Aperture, Inc., publishes a periodical, portfolios and books to communicate with serious photographers and creative people everywhere. A complete catalogue will be mailed upon request. Address: Elm Street, Millerton, New York 12546.

All rights reserved under International and Pan-American Copyright Conventions. Published in the United States by Aperture, Inc., and simultaneously in France by Robert Delpire, Éditeur, Paris, in Great Britain by Gordon Fraser Gallery, Ltd., London.

Library of Congress Catalogue Card No. 77-70070

ISBN: 0-912334-96-7

Manufactured in the United States of America.

André Kertész's pictures are deceptively simple. They are devoid of extravagance, of excess, and of artificiality. And astonishingly they have been so from the very beginning. Through more than sixty years Kertész has worked without pretense, in self-observation, using the camera to question, to record, and to preserve his relationship to the world and to his art. He has remained true to his own way of seeing, and as a result his art and his life have been inextricably bound together in his photographs.

Though as a youth he had no pretensions about making "great art," Kertész nevertheless got off on the right foot when he determined to please himself. He could easily have imitated the photographs of the early twentieth-century soft-focus salon portraits and landscapes, but he realized intuitively that such pictures tampered with the real nature of their subjects. From the start he was more interested in depicting facts than in inventing fictions.

This task was not an easy one. Kertész was drawn not to particularly lofty subjects, but rather toward representing the true and fragile nature of the existing world without altering it. The camera was the perfect instrument, a seemingly dispassionate recorder reaching toward reality. And so Kertész, long before photography was a fashionable profession, and against his family's preference that he become a banker, set out to look at the world and to contemplate it with the greatest attention and respect. At first he would explore; innovation was to follow.

It was 1912 when he bought his first camera, an ICA box-type. For the next thirteen years he photographed people he met by chance and those he knew well, places he frequented, and events, such as World War I, in which he was at once an involved participant and an objective observer. Except for those of the war, his early pictures were taken mostly in and around Budapest, his birthplace. Though many of them were lost in the Hungarian Revolution of 1918, the few that survive show his disinterest in the drama and elegance of the city that was called "the Paris of Central Europe." Instead, he ruthlessly chose to record the simple, quintessential Hungarian moments that he deeply felt.

As he explored his everyday world, he came, probably without realizing it, to have another subject: photography itself. He loved the medium's versatility, and he tried everything. Instead of working only on bright, clear days, he photographed in all kinds of weather—anxious to see what the camera recorded when it rained or snowed, when there was an abundance of light or a virtual lack of it. In one early picture (1921), dark figures lurch across the wet cobblestone streets of a Budapest square drenched by a sudden spring shower. In another, taken on an autumn afternoon, a single horse-drawn cart pushes its way through the heavy November fog. Others were taken on snowy days; many, at night. He also concerned himself with time—not just with freezing the significant moment, but with capturing the sense of time passing, the act unfolding, the feeling of movement.

He found no need to manufacture pictures or to force responses when the richness of the world was so plainly visible, and the camera so capable of capturing it. Thus his pictures began to take individual form, to record what his eye instinctively found to see. As such, they were not crystal-clear renditions of the world. Visually, abstractions began to take shape as photographic detail was sacrificed to capture the essence of a moment. These were the fruits not of happy accident, but of conscious choice.

In 1925 Kertész left Budapest for Paris. The move was a manifesto, a natural, well-timed declaration, and only in the smallest sense was it a risk. The time had come for him to exchange a shaky business career for that of a committed artist. Since 1912 he had been photographing whenever he could, in between jobs at the Stock Exchange. His photographs had been published in the illustrated Hungarian magazines. He was thirty-one years old, sufficiently confident of his abilities, clearly aware of his own value, and ambitious to extend his limits. In Hungary he lacked the supportive atmosphere of an artistic community; in Paris, perhaps, he could live his life rather than continually have to explain it.

Kertész had intuitively grasped that the camera could be used in direct response to how he felt about the world; now he was ready to explore his art on another level. In Paris he was able to give reign to his intellectual, even analytical and self-conscious sense of form. In the same way as he had roamed the Budapest countryside, he stalked the streets of Paris. He pointed his camera everywhere: upwards across rooftops, into windows, taking in entire façades or selecting out small details; downwards onto sidewalks speckled with people working themselves into patterns, merging with cement curbs, cobblestones, edges of trees, and slices of buildings. Vantage point became important. And each time he made a picture he learned a bit more about the city that was now his home.

Everything seemed to work for him. Even though a photographer ranked, perhaps, with a gypsy fortuneteller in this art capital of the world, when the artists of Paris saw Kertész's work there was a stirring of interest. And it was they who were the first to recognize his unconventional pictures.

His first show was in 1927 at the Sacre du Printemps, a small, innovative modern art gallery on the Left Bank. The critics were generous in their praise, and Kertész was invited to show in the First Independent Salon of Photography. He was courted by editors and virtually given his choice of assignments. His free-lance reporting paid his way. He exhibited, published books (three in as many years), and was a major contributor to the leading German magazines (*Frankfurter illustrierte* and *Berliner illustrierte*) and to their French counterparts (*Vu* and *Art et Médecine*). European museums began to collect his work. By the time he was forty years old, in 1934, he was venerated as a master of the photographic medium.

His friends in Paris were the revolutionary artists of their day: Mondrian, Léger, Chagall, Vlaminck, Lurçat, Calder, Eisenstein—each in revolt against art, morality, and society. And Kertész joined them in the celebration that was Paris between two world wars. Quickly he was accepted as a member of the avant-garde scene that centered around Montparnasse. It was a spontaneous life, a happy one that seemed all the more intense because art and life were so pressed together.

For a short time he worked on a series of nude distortions that he had begun in Hungary years before. Eventually he determined that he could see no further development in the work. Still, there were over 150 innovative pictures that were rich in their surrealistic qualities. Even more than in his street pictures, there was a sense of life as a dream. The surrealistic concept of transforming reality into fantasy made its way into Kertész's technique. His work came to influence his friends' paintings.

As he was stimulated by the ideas of artists around him, his pictures grew less sentimental and more sophisticated. They became highly refined, sensitive observations of the abstract relationships between curves, angles, light, and shadow. And because of his sensitivity they were as beautiful, or surprising, or whimsical as they were firmly rooted in the everyday world. It was an atmosphere in which Kertész thrived.

In 1937 Kertész decided, against the advice of friends, to leave Paris for New York City to work on a contract he had been offered by Keystone Studios, a major picture agency of the time. When he terminated the contract with Keystone eight months later, World War II was pending; a return to Paris was not only impractical but impossible. For the first time in his life there was no choice: America was to become home, at least temporarily.

Kertész, with his reputation, his portfolio of pictures and books haphazardly collected for the trip, was eager to work. He found himself in a country that was excited by photography as a means of personal expression and as a modern means of communication. His talent as a major

European photographer and his understanding of subjective reportage with a 35mm camera should have guaranteed him employment. But from the beginning his European sensibilities were to clash with those of the American editors excited by their own talent for invention, and with earnest young museum directors making their first attempts at accounting for the phenomenon of photography—a medium in which Kertész had worked for some twenty years.

He was told by the editors of *Life,* when he visited their offices, that his pictures "spoke too much." What they meant was, his work did not need their highly polished words. It was profoundly symbolical, whereas *Life* wanted to pinpoint the world clearly in its readers' minds almost as though it were a newspaper. Moreover, when shooting for European picture magazines (the prototypes for *Life*), Kertész had always managed to cover the assignments in six to twelve pictures. Such frugality only squelched the *Life* editors, who were accustomed to a wide sample from which to select the right picture to combine with the right words. This relationship was totally at odds. It could satisfy neither party, and so Kertész never worked for *Life.*

Yet photography by 1937 had indeed arrived in America. That year Edward Weston received the first Guggenheim grant ever given to a photographic artist, and Weston himself exemplified the American photographic movement. His approach to picture-making was direct. It was a relationship founded on respect, at the very least, and perhaps love of the mechanistic characteristics of photography. Unlike Kertész, who worked gingerly with a 35mm camera, Weston used a large-format camera, the smallest aperture opening, and long exposures. Thus he was able to achieve photographs characterized by unusual depth of field and brilliant definition of detail. Kertész, on the other hand, never cared for extreme sharpness or for definition of detail. His choice of the 35mm camera enabled him to capture the expression of the moment. Although both Weston and Kertész allowed the subject its own authority, each came to the subject with an altogether different set of sensibilities. If Weston's rendition of the world was epic and his clean, unblurred pictures awesome, Kertész's work was consistently moving because his photographs mirrored the fragile, evolving nature of all human experience.

So Kertész, whose photographs were too subjective and evocative for the picture magazines of the day, found himself out of step, for neither did he fit in with the community of American photographic artists who were set on defining a highly intellectual, peculiarly American aesthetic.

Although the first major photography show at The Museum of Modern Art in 1937, "Photography, 1848–1937," represented Kertész by five photographs, it was to be his last until 1946, when the Chicago Art Institute honored him with a one-man show. He had come to America when the country was getting acquainted with photography, but he would have to wait until the Americans found their sure footing in photographic terms. Then, decades later, they would turn to him, demanding to know where he'd been all along. They would discover him for themselves.

During those years in between, Kertész free-lanced for *Harper's Bazaar, Vogue, Town & Country, Collier's, Coronet,* and *Look.* Eventually he signed an exclusive contract with Condé Nast Publications, which provided a livelihood for him and his wife, Elizabeth, over the next thirteen years. He continued working isolated from the mainstream of critical acceptance. He became a master at straddling both worlds. When he did commercial assignments for *House & Garden,* he also carried his Leica. During breaks in the shooting sessions, he made his own pictures. In short, he survived. Under these conditions, although he did not add substantially to his major body of work, his eye did not move from its belief.

Kertész was seventy years old when in the 1960's American curators finally took note of his presence. John Szarkowski mounted a major one-man show at The Museum of Modern Art in 1964. Thus began a series of exhibitions which have continued into this decade. Kertész at last had come into his own.

Although Kertész's world has been in a continual state of flux, the center of that world—his one-to-one relationship with his subjects and his art—has remained secure. Never did he veer from that truthful plane in order to please his peers or to elicit recognition. His photographs, then, reveal a whole world at once expected and unexpected to anyone who examines them.

Carole Kismaric

11

17

41

43

PHOTOGRAPHS

HONORS CONFERRED UPON ANDRÉ KERTÉSZ

Silver medal at the Exposition Coloniale, Paris, 1930; gold medal at the IVth Mostra Biennale Internazionale della Fotografia, Venice, Italy, 1962; honorary member of the American Society of Magazine Photographers and guest of honor at the Miami Conference on Communication Arts, University of Miami, Florida, 1965; Commander of the Order of Arts and Letters (from the French government), 1976.

BRIEF CHRONOLOGY

1894. André Kertész born July 2, Budapest, Hungary.

1912. Receives baccalaureate from Academy of Commerce, Budapest; works as clerk in Budapest Stock Exchange. Buys first camera, ICA box-type, and photographs candid street scenes, genre subjects.

1914–18. Serves in Austro-Hungarian army; wounded in 1915. Makes photographs of war and the communes with Goerz Tenax camera.

1916. Receives prize for satiric self-portrait from *Borsszem Janko* magazine.

1917. Publishes photographs in *Erdekes Ujsag* magazine.

1925–28. Moves to Paris. Free-lances for *Frankfurter illustrierte, UHU* magazine, *Berliner illustrierte, Strassburger illustrierte, Le Nazione Fiorenze, Vu,* London *Times,* among other publications.

1927. Buys first Leica.

1929. Photographs are purchased for collections of Staaliche Museen Kunstbibliothek, Berlin, and Konig-Albert Museum, Zwickau.

1930. *Art et Médecine* begins publication; Kertész is a major contributor until 1936.

1936. Arrives in New York under contract to Keystone Studios.

1937. Terminates studio contract.

1937–49. Free-lances for *Harper's Bazaar, Vogue, Town & Country, American Magazine, Collier's, Coronet, Look.*

1944. Becomes American citizen.

1949–62. Signs exclusive contract with Condé Nast publications; terminates contract after thirteen years.

Since 1962, Kertész has worked for himself. He has published numerous books and has been honored at exhibitions throughout the world.

MAJOR EXHIBITIONS

1928. One-man show, Sacre du Printemps Gallery, Paris, March 12, 1928; exhibit, First Independent Salon of Photography, Paris.

1932. Thirty-five prints, exhibition of modern European photography, Julien Levy Gallery, New York City.

1934. Group show, Leleu's, Paris; group show, Galerie de la Pléiade, Paris.

1946. One-man show, Art Institute, Chicago.

1962. One-man show, Long Island University, New York; IVth Mostra Biennale Internazionale della Fotografia, Venice.

1963. One-man show, Bibliothèque Nationale, Paris.

1964–65. One-man show, Museum of Modern Art, New York City.

1967. Group show, "The Concerned Photographer," Riverside Museum, New York City.

1970. Exhibit of ten photographs, U.S. Pavilion, World's Fair Expo, Tokyo, Japan.

1971. One-man show, Moderna Museet, Stockholm; one-man show, Magyar Nemzeti Galeria, Budapest.

1972. One-man show, Valokuvamuseon, Helsinki.

1973. One-man show, Hallmark Gallery, New York City.

1976. One-man show, Wesleyan University, Middletown, Connecticut; one-man show, French Cultural Services, New York City.

BOOKS BY ANDRÉ KERTÉSZ

1933. *Enfants.* Sixty photographs of children. Text by Jaboune. Paris: Éditions d'Histoire et d'Art.

1934. *Paris vu par André Kertész.* Text by Pierre Mac Orlan. Paris: Éditions d'Histoire et d'Art, Librairie Plon. 46 pages.

1936. *Nos amies les bêtes par André Kertész.* Text by Jaboune. Paris: Éditions d'Histoire et d'Art, Librairie Plon. 48 pages.

1937. *Les cathédrales du vin.* Text by Pierre Hamp. Paris: Établissements Sainrapt et Brice (3,100 copies). 28 pages.

1945. *Day of Paris.* George Davis, editor. New York: J. J. Augustin. 146 pages.

1971. *On Reading.* New York: Grossman Publishers. 64 pages.

1972. *André Kertész: Sixty Years of Photography, 1912–1972.* Edited by Nicolas Ducrot. New York: Grossman Publishers. 224 pages.

1974. *J'aime Paris: Photographs Since the Twenties.* Edited by Nicolas Ducrot. New York: Grossman Publishers, a division of Viking Press. 224 pages.

1975. *Washington Square.* Introduction by Brendan Gill. New York: Grossman Publishers, a division of Viking Press. 96 pages.

1976. *Distortions.* Introduction by Hilton Kramer. New York: Alfred A. Knopf. Unpaged, 200 photographs. *Of New York.* New York: Alfred A. Knopf. 192 pages.

ARTICLES ABOUT ANDRÉ KERTÉSZ

Pierre Bost, "Le Salon des indépendants de la photographie." *La revue hebdomadaire et son supplément illustré,* No. 24 (1928).

Brassaï, "My Friend André Kertész." *Camera,* No. 4 (1963). "Caricatures and Distortions." *Encyclopedia of Photography,* Greistan Press.

Owen Edwards, "Zen and the Art of Photography." *The Village Voice* (April 5, 1976).

Anna Fárová, *André Kertész—Photographic Series.* New York: Grossman Publishers (1966).

Lois Greenfield, "Kertész: Discovered at 70." *Changes* (April, 1975).

Hilton Kramer, "Kertész Conveys Poetic Significance of Details." New York *Times* (January 17, 1973).

————, "Two Masters of Photography." New York *Times* (March 27, 1976).

Zay Laslo, "Az Ember A Kep Eṡ A Muveszet." *Foto,* No. 6 (1971).

Pierre Mac Orlan, "La photographie et le fantastique social." *Les Annales,* Paris (March, 1927).

Janet Malcolm, "On and Off the Avenue." *The New Yorker* (May 1, 1971).

Carlo Rim, "Défense et illustration de la photographie." *Vu,* Paris (April 20, 1932).

————, "Grandeur et servitude du reporter photographie." *Marianne,* Paris (February 21, 1934).

Leo Rubinfein, "André Kertész: French Cultural Services." *Artforum* (Summer, 1976).

John Szarkowski, "André Kertész, Photographer." Museum of Modern Art, New York City. Recension of catalogue and exhibition: London *Times* (March 25, 1965).

Margaret R. Weiss, "André Kertész, Photographer." *Saturday Review* (December 20, 1964).